BEAUTY IN THE LIGHT OF THE REDEMPTION

BEAUTY IN THE LIGHT OF THE REDEMPTION

DIETRICH VON HILDEBRAND

HILDEBRAND
PROJECT

First Edition

Published 2019 by Hildebrand Press
1235 University Blvd., Steubenville, Ohio 43952

Publisher's Cataloguing-in-Publication Information

Von Hildebrand, Dietrich, 1889–1977.
Beauty in the light of the redemption / by Dietrich von Hildebrand.
Steubenville, OH: Hildebrand Press, 2019.
Subjects: LCSH Aesthetics. | Art—Philosophy. | Christianity and art.
| Phenomenology. | BISAC PHILOSOPHY / Aesthetics | PHILOSOPHY /
Aesthetics | PHILOSOPHY / Movements / Phenomenology | RELIGION /
Christianity / Literature & the Arts
Classification: LCC B3359 .V6 2019 | DDC 701—dc23

ISBN 978-1-939773-05-0
LCCN 2019907731

Set in Monotype Perpetua, a typeface designed by English sculptor Eric Gill
Typeset by Kachergis Book Design

Front Cover Font: Hoefler Text
Cover Image: The Fighting Temeraire, by J.M.W Turner, in the
National Gallery (London)
Image from Wikimedia Commons

Production and Cover Design by Christopher T. Haley

We acknowledge Rick and Vera Hough, whose generous support has made possible the publication of this book.

www.hildebrandproject.org

CONTENTS

BEAUTY IN THE LIGHT OF THE REDEMPTION

What importance is to be attributed to beauty in the life of a Christian? What role *should* it play in the life of those who have been redeemed? What is the relationship between redemption and beauty? Did beauty lose its significance after the redemption?

Here we are not speaking of beauty in the general sense of the word or, as I may say, about metaphysical beauty. When we are profoundly affected by the beauty of purity, when the Church in her liturgy exclaims, "How beautiful is the chaste generation with splendour," or, again, when we speak of the beauty acquired by a soul through humility, then

This essay first appeared in 1951 in the *Journal of Arts and Letters* under the title "Beauty and the Christian." It appeared subsequently under its present title in *The New Tower of Babel* (1953) and, in German translation, in *Die Menschheit am Scheideweg* (1954).

we are concentrating on metaphysical beauty, which is an aura, a refulgence, a radiance of the inner qualities of these virtues. It is a beauty which St. Augustine calls "*splendor veri*," and which is, as it were, a radiation of every genuine quality that adheres to every good in the sum of its qualities.

This beauty is not our problem. Its relationship to the redemption, its function in the life of the Christian is not problematic. The liturgy leaves no doubt in our minds as to the role due to this beauty in the light of revelation. Again and again it is spoken of in a great variety of phrases, thus:

> "Listen, daughter, and see, and incline thine ear, for the king has greatly desired thy beauty."
>
> "Give ear with thy countenance and thy beauty."
>
> "Beautiful in countenance and more beautiful in faith."

There are many similar references in the liturgy. This beauty is not to be severed from the quality, whose reflection and aura it is. Therefore, it naturally has a conspicuous function in the life of the Christian, for this beauty is the foundation of love. The divine beauty of Jesus, the beauty of the Saint of all saints, inflames our heart. It shone resplendent on the apostles on Tabor; the beauty of His divine mercy melted the heart of Mary Magdalen. The irresistible divine beauty of Jesus not only moves our will, but it attracts our heart; as St. Augustine says, "We are attracted not only by the will but also by affection."

The great Lacordaire says that virtues become irresistibly victorious and constrain us to love only when, as in every saint, they are manifested in their beauty, when their inner nobility is revealed in their beauty.

In its dignity, this beauty, which is the reflection of the inner excellence and dignity of one who exists, is dependent on the dignity of the object. The beauty of a rich, profound mind like that of a Plato or an Aristotle is greater than the beauty of an Achilles, which is peculiar to the vital fullness of an exuberant vigor, and the beauty of humility or love is greater than that of an eminent and profound intellect.

The status of this beauty with regard to the redemption, as we have already said, is not our problem, nor is this beauty really our primary theme. The beauty of humility is not the primary theme of humility, just as the beauty of truth is not the primary theme of truth. It is an excess, yet connected essentially with these values, an efflorescence of them, their quintessence, their "countenance." Therefore, it is so much a part of redemption, that redemption is also a restoration of the original paradisaical beauty, of an even much greater beauty, as the liturgy maintains: "Who has wonderfully created human dignity and more wonderfully restored it"; and as a mystic says: "We would die of love if we could see the beauty of a soul in the state of grace."

Our problem is concerned with beauty in a narrower sense of the word, with beauty that radiates from visible and audible things. It is the beauty that unfolds before us when we look out from the Capitoline Hill upon the Roman Forum with the Campagna and the Alban Hill in the distance, or the beauty of the Medici tombs by Michelangelo, or the beauty that is revealed when we listen to Beethoven's ninth symphony. It is the beauty of the visible and the audible with which we have contact in nature and in art, which, for want of another expression, we shall call the beauty of form by way of contrast with metaphysical beauty.

What is the relationship of *this* beauty to the redemption? What is its status in the life of the Christian? What importance is due to it in the light of revelation and of our transformation in Christ? Some maintain that beauty of form belongs to the sphere of luxury, to that part of life that, in the light of Christ, cannot make demands in real earnest. Certainly, it is nothing wicked but something innocent. But to these people the question whether a building is beautiful or not, whether there is one work of art more or less, is really something secondary and external. They argue that for the aesthetes and pagans it may seem like something great and important; for the Christian who, with holy sobriety, knows that the serious things of life are to be sought in the moral and social fields, beauty of form is something relatively trifling and unimportant. Certainly, they say, it belongs to human life as do amusements and games of every kind. It is, however, much more important that a knife cut well than that it have a pleasing appearance. It is more important that a person have a roof over his head than that his house merely satisfy an exquisitely artistic taste. They believe that art, the whole cultivation of beauty of form, is something only for the upper ten thousand after all. This consideration in itself proves that beauty of form is something that does not really belong to the seriousness of existence. In former ages of princely courts and of feudal organizations, the whole cult of the beautiful flourished; our times are too serious for that. They conclude that today the Christian must concentrate upon great economic, political, and social problems. Love of a neighbor must show him that it is much more important for every person to maintain an existence worthy of a human being, that the sick and the poor must be cared for, than it is to hang a beautiful picture some place or other or to have *Figaro* brilliantly performed. They apply the same criterion to churches. Of importance are the tabernacle, the altar, the Holy Sacrifice that is celebrated there, for which a structure must be provided. Whether this structure be beautiful or not is secondary. Only aesthetes can find this essential. Therefore, in the minds of these individuals, beauty of form in the light of Christ is something unessential and destitute of genuine seriousness; so much so, that there might even be the danger of weakening us, of making sensualists of us, of turning us away from the real duties of a Christian and from those things that, from the viewpoint of Christian charity, are indispensable. In the life of the Christian it should, therefore, play a secondary role.

Respondeo:

This utilitarianism is by no means the spirit of the Gospel. Certainly, in the light of the *unum necessarium*, our eternal salvation, beauty of form is secondary, but this is equally true of economic and social problems. Does not our Lord say, "Therefore be not solicitous saying, what shall we eat or what shall we drink or wherewith shall we be clothed"? In the light of the Gospel, then, it is not possible to play off the "useful" and practically obligatory things of life against the beautiful by emphasizing the fact that beauty of form does not belong to the *unum necessarium*, for this is also valid for the sphere of the "useful." It is, rather, of consequence to understand that practical and absolute necessity is not the only standard for the value of things. Christ's saying, "Man does not live by bread alone," is to be applied, in the first place, to the religious sphere. However, it can also justly be extended to every spiritual realm.

An estimate of all things from the viewpoint of their practical and absolute necessity, restriction to that which is absolutely necessary, a spirit that is legitimately master of the technical sciences, is to be found neither in God's creation nor in the revelation of Christ. In these, on the contrary, the principle of superabundance rules. Is God not lavish in His creation? Do we not meet this divine profusion in the realm of propagation? Is beauty in nature not the clearest proof of this divine profusion, since it is in no way practically indispensable in the economy of nature? Is creation itself, as such, not the fruit of this divine profusion? Is it not the pure emanation of the infinite love of God and in no way necessary? The first miracle of Christ at the wedding feast in Cana reveals to us in a glorious manner the superabundance of divine love, which shows no restriction to that which is necessary. The wine was not at all indispensable for the wedding feast. It was not even entirely wanting, but there was simply lacking a sufficiency. Certainly, the primary purpose of this miracle was the manifestation of Christ's divinity, but it is a fact that the content of the miracle has reference only to heightening the resplendence of the feast, not a radical renunciation of all forms of utilitarianism. And when our Lord says, “The poor you have always with you, but Me you have not always,” may we not discover in His words a Magna Carta for the importance that should be conceded to beauty? Is the ointment, whose waste was criticized by the apostles, not an exalted symbol of the things that, without being indispensable, are yet good and pleasing to God? No, the indispensability of a thing is *one* point of view, the value of a thing another. The fact that beauty of form is not indispensable does not affect its value and its importance. Later we will speak of the deep significance that dwells in beauty of form.

Sometimes, however, we hear objections to beauty of form that are to be taken more seriously. Certain individuals say that it is something external, that it is attached to material and corporal objects, to that which is visible and audible. It is, therefore, much more external and less sublime, to say the least, than metaphysical beauty that, for example, is attached to the beauty of truth or of virtue, as we have mentioned above.

Beauty of form is certainly something that belongs to the realm of the senses and is, therefore, necessarily something relatively inferior within the compass of that which exists. May it, for this reason, still claim to have an important function in the life of the Christian? Does not all asceticism strive toward a detachment from the senses, to draw us back more and more into our spiritual nature, to become indifferent to that which pleases the senses and to advance beyond? Does not this beauty, therefore, also belong to the specially mundane things that, without being evil, yet divert us from God, from the Kingdom of God, and from our eternal destiny? Does not much become sweet for mystics, that was bitter to the senses, and much bitter that was sweet to the senses? Does it not belong to the revolution of revelation, to the new eyes with which we are to behold everything according to the redemption, that this beauty of form loses its significance, that it proves to be one of the *vanitates* of the earth, as we read in the Book of Wisdom, "Appearance is deceitful and beauty is vain." Is this beauty, consequently, not something specially *mundane*? In itself it is something absolutely positive, nothing wicked; yet, is it not perishable, attached to the perishable? Is it not something that loses its significance the more we are united with God, the more we live in Christ "through Him, with Him, and in Him"? Does not our Lord say to Martha, "Martha, Martha, you are worried and troubled over many things, one thing alone is necessary"? Is this not also valid in the case of beauty of form in nature and art? For a pagan who recognizes only natural goods, whose mind is entirely directed toward earthly things, this beauty may be the goal; for him, however, who has been illuminated by the light of Christ, it can no longer be essential. Neither is this beauty indispensable for sanctity. The question of St. Aloysius, "What does this avail for eternity?", is incompatible with beauty of form. Must we not admit, then, that it is rather an obstacle in the process of dying to ourselves and of being transformed in Christ, and that it has, consequently, lost its significance through the redemption?

Respondeo:

No. This concept is erroneous, and the error can be attributed to a multiform misunderstanding of the essence of beauty of form. The comprehension of this beauty presupposes the use of the senses. A blind person cannot grasp the beauty of Bernini's Colonnade or that of the Church of San Marco in

Venice. A deaf person cannot be moved by Beethoven's *Missa Solemnis* or by one of his quartets. It is necessary, in cases such as these, to understand the function of the senses as well as the relationship of these visible and audible objects to their beauty. Although beauty of form presupposes sight and hearing, yet, in itself, it is by no means something belonging to the realm of the senses, something, as it were, congenial with this realm which bears the stamp of the corporeal-sensible. In the concept mentioned above, beauty of form was spoken of as if it were a pleasurable sensation of the eye and the ear. That is, manifestly, a gross error. If a light blinds me, my senses experience displeasure, yet no one will say that this light is ugly or in bad taste. If I behold something indistinctly or with great effort, perhaps with spectacles that are no good, then this is a displeasure for my eyes, but that which I see does not necessarily thereby become ugly; when I put on good spectacles and experience the clear and distinct vision as a pleasure, then that which I see can be ugly, base, or trivial, and appear to me to be so. The same is true for the ear. That which is pleasant or unpleasant to the senses is congenial with the sphere of the senses; it bears the stamp of the incorporally apparent; it is not, however, beauty or ugliness, which are clearly distinct from these sense experiences. The pleasure and the displeasure of my eyes are experienced in connection with my body; it is a sense experience. The beauty of the Palazzo Farnese, however, certainly has nothing to do with my body, and its comprehension is separated by a world from sense perception. It is also characteristic that beauty of form be found only in the realm of the visible and audible and not in the sphere of smell, taste, and touch. Even though there is, without a doubt, not only the difference of pleasant and unpleasant, but also such qualities as ordinary, rich, delicate in these latter, yet here we cannot speak of beauty in the full sense of the word. That is due to the fact that beauty is not attached to mere realities of sense but in definite visible and audible creations, which, even as such, represent something much more differentiated, more richly constructed and formed. Fragrances cannot fashion a new product as tones do a melody. Briefly, beauty of form is not sensuous like the agreeable taste of food, and it does not, therefore, bear the stamp of the corporeal like these.

It is not sufficient, however, to distinguish beauty of form from the sensation of pleasure in the senses; within this beauty itself we must make some important distinctions.

There are two kinds of beauty of form. One of them is comparatively primitive as, for example, the beauty of a circle as opposed to an arbitrarily irregular figure, the beauty of a clear musical note as opposed to a noise, a chord as opposed to a discord, or the beauty of certain faces with regular features, let us say "Hollywood-beauty." This beauty, though it is no mere pleasure for the eyes, is still comparatively close to the world of the senses. The other is an immeasurably higher one. It demands not only the coordination of many more factors, but, qualitatively, it is something entirely new. It is the beauty that unfolds before us when, on a glorious day, we look out from the Janiculum upon Rome and the mountains beyond, or when we contemplate the *Creation of Adam* by Michelangelo in the Sistine Chapel, or when we are uniquely absorbed in Mozart's *Don Giovanni*. This beauty, wherever it appears, calls into being in our minds a whole spiritual world that is laden with a host of spiritual elements: the poetic as opposed to the prosaic, necessity as opposed to arbitrariness, inner abundance as opposed to every falsehood and affectation, inner greatness as opposed to everything mediocre, breadth and depth as opposed to all that is insipid and trivial.

Our problem has reference to this sublimely higher beauty of form, which so evidently rises above the world of the sensuous and discloses a sublime incorporeality, and about which it is impossible to say that it is directed to the lower part of our soul. What is the position of this beauty of form with reference to the redemption?

Attempts to rescue the incorporeality of this beauty of form by maintaining that it is not at all attached to the visible and audible have not been wanting. Ideas or thoughts, to which the audible and visible stimulate us, are the true bearers. If, for example, we view a lofty mountain range bathed in gleaming sunlight, it is not that which we see directly before us to which beauty is attached, but the thought of God's creative power is the real beauty. In a word, the real bearer of beauty is something incorporeal that we connect intellectually with the visible and audible by means of analogies; or, it is said, the visible has a function similar to that of the symbol in the liturgy. This attempt at rescuing the incorporeality of beauty is well meant, to be sure, but it is false, for the beauty of the Campagna Romana or that of the seventh symphony by Bruckner is intuitive, linked directly with that which is seen and heard, and no intellectual ascent to something else is necessary in order to grasp this beauty. We must not try to evade the mysteries in reality, but in a complete *thaumazein* at the mystery, we must try to understand it by means of a deeper penetration. This higher beauty of form is also bestowed directly and intuitively by means of the visible and the audible, and in spite of its connection with the senses, it is of a spiritual sublimity that qualitatively completely transcends the sphere of the senses. How can this be explained?

This beauty (and we here arrive at one of the most important points) adheres directly to the visible and audible, to be sure, but it is not *the expression of the essence* of these visible and audible objects as is metaphysical beauty. It is on a much lower plane and could not explain the sublimity of beauty of form. This higher beauty of form in its quality transcends by far the sphere of these objects. The beauty of the Bay of Naples is of the highest incorporeality and does not speak of that which mountains, trees, water signify ontologically, nor of that which they signify to a scientist or a philosopher of nature, but of a higher world that is reflected in it. It is a great mystery that God has entrusted to visible and audible capacities: to be able to place before us sublime, spiritual qualities, a beauty that, in its quality, reflects God's world, and that speaks of this higher transfigured world. The function of the senses and of the visible and audible capacities in this is of a modest, humble kind; they are a pedestal, a mirror for something much higher. Therefore, this beauty in its dignity is not bound to the ontological dignity of the object. As a consequence, a flower is incomparably more beautiful than a worm; a Monte Pellegrino in Palermo, bathed in a sunset glow, is more beautiful than an animal, though the animal ranks higher ontologically. As soon as we understand that beauty of form (to be sure, adhering directly intuitively to the visible and audible and in no way a result of reflections, analogies, or symbolic connections) is not due to the object in the same manner or does not speak of it, but is the ontological reflection of something incomparably higher, then we will also understand that it is absolutely false to designate it as sensuous, external, and particularly *mundane*. The beauty of the Italian landscape, of Tuscan villas, of

Assisi, the beauty of the *Tempesta* by Giorgione, the frescoes of Masaccio in the Carmine, the beauty of the dome of Florence or of St. Peter's, the beauty of the first chorale in Bach's *St. Matthew Passion*, or of Mozart's *Figaro*—all these are, to be sure, immediately attached to audible and visible things; they are not connected with beauty of form merely by thoughts; they are not ideas that these express thereby, but in their quality they speak about another, higher reality—they make God known.

The elements upon which beauty of form depends, that is, when and under what circumstances it appears in visible and audible objects, are multiform and mysterious. There is no recipe, nor could anyone make rules to be followed to create something beautiful. Every individual case must have new individual inspiration. One thing, however, we can determine, that the conditions be in the sphere of the visible and audible, like proportion, composition, harmony, rhythm, etc.

Here there is again revealed the whole mystery of the beauty of form, the transcendence in this sphere. Conditions, which are apparently trifling and external, have a strongly, profoundly, and significantly spiritual effect. It depends on outward conditions, so to speak, when a window opens, but that which we see through the window when it is once open is weighty, significant, and by no means external. Again and again it is necessary to understand the mystery of this beauty of form. It is directly attached to visible and audible things, but the reality about which it speaks qualitatively, the substance, whose quintessence it is, is a spiritual world which towers high above everything corporeal. This must also be brought out distinctly in the answer we give. The metaphysical beauty of a saint awakens in us a desire for closer association with him, for we know that this beauty is a reflection of his personality.

With beauty of form, on the contrary, it is otherwise. The beauty of Monte Pellegrino in Palermo does not arouse the desire in us to caress it, but, as we behold its beauty, our heart is filled with a desire for loftier regions about which this beauty speaks, and it looks upward with longing. In order to behold this beauty, we need not know God, much less think of Him, for, objectively, there is a reflection of God in these things, not merely in the manner with which all that exists portrays God, but by having something *appear* in things of a relatively low ontological rank, which in a special manner announces

God in its quality. Only when we have understood this quasi-sacramental function of the visible and audible, this mystery that God has entrusted to it, can we do justice to the function of this beauty in the life of the redeemed. It is not true that this beauty distracts us from God and is specifically mundane. On the contrary, it contains a summons; in it there dwells a *sursum corda*; it awakens awe in us; it elevates us above that which is base; it fills our hearts with a longing for the eternal beauty of God.

A misunderstanding also arises from the fact that all beauty is seen in the light of the beauty of the human face or body, and from the moral danger that can emanate from this, conclusions are drawn about the "sensuality" of all beauty of form. These are, manifestly, false deductions. This beauty is accidentally attached to things that can appeal to the sensual appetites. It is possible that here beauty of form can psychologically aggravate the kindling of the sensual appetites; in the case of the beauty of a landscape, a work of art, a symphony, it can no longer come into question. To see beauty of form, in general, as an arousing of the sensual appetites is nonsense. If anyone has a feeling for it, there resounds a sublime voice from above in the beauty of the adagio of Beethoven's ninth symphony; its quality speaks of a world of purity and incorporeality; and he who hears it senses the incompatibility of all that is base and morally bad with this world. Yes, the exalted beauty of form is so far removed from drawing us down into the "world and its pomp," that there is a profound connection between this beauty and the realm of moral values. The breath of a more exalted world, which dwells in beauty of form, is also a *sursum corda* from the moral point of view.

Neither has all this been left behind and discarded by the redemption. On the contrary, our relationship with all this beauty of form in nature and in art, to be sure, becomes something *different* and something new in Christ and through Christ, as does the relationship with all created values; however, it does not grow less but becomes more profound and much greater.

Here we come upon a mysterious paradox: the more we give ourselves entirely to God, the more we love God above all else, the deeper and truer is our love for all created things that really deserve our love. The inordinate attachment to earthly possessions, which can even degenerate into idolatry, is not a greater love, but a lesser, impure, perverted one.

The love of creatures, whether it be father, friend, or wife, can reach its full measure only in Christ, only by loving them in Christ and with Christ, indeed, only by partaking of the same love with which Christ loves them.

Thus, the sense of this natural, qualitative message from God is not suppressed by the redemption; it is set aright and transfigured by Christ. In all this beauty, which makes God known objectively, the redeemed will also consciously find God; he will draw out the line away back to its source; he will, indeed, seek and find in all the sublime beauty of the visible and audible world the Countenance and the Voice of the God-Man, Christ. The beauty of a landscape, of a great work of art is, thus, no less estimable, but, on the contrary, its comprehension is immeasurably more profound; it discloses *more* than it would to the eyes of the aesthete who idolizes it with an inordinate love. All possessions that appeal to our pride and our sensual appetites, indeed, all that are subjectively gratifying, lose their radiance for the redeemed, for the man, who has found the pearl of great price of the Gospel. All possessions, however, that have real value, that in themselves are honorable, excellent, significant, that fall like dew from above and ascend to God like incense, achieve a higher and new radiance in Christ. It is true that beauty of form does not belong to the *unum necessarium*; it is true that a person who has no feeling for it or who admires trivial and bad art can also become a saint and enter into heaven, just as one who is incapable of grasping philosophical truths and of distinguishing them from philosophical errors, who is intellectually limited and weak, could yet become a saint. However, merely because something is indispensable, it is not thereby prevented from possessing a profound and exalted value.

It is true that beauty of form does not belong to that which we must seek before all else. "Seek ye first the kingdom of God and His justice, and all these things will be added unto you" applies here also. This does not mean, however, that all else is useless. In this case, also, we must not say that the redeemed do not seek beauty of form before all else, but that they are first seeking the Kingdom of God, and in the same measure as they do so, will they more and more appreciate this great gift of God and understand it. St. Francis of Assisi reveals this so beautifully. How profoundly did he grasp the beauty of form in nature. How mysteriously did he, who sought only the Kingdom of God (I venture to say, *because* he sought the Kingdom of God), inspire the art and poetry of the thirteenth, fourteenth, and fifteenth centuries. How greatly did his spirit become the seed for one of the most important periods of florescence in art.

To the eyes of him who is redeemed, however, not only are deeper dimensions of the beauty of form revealed; he also understands clearly the significance of the beauty of form in his life. He understands, first of all, that God is glorified by things with beauty of form. He understands how greatly the world has been enriched by a Mozart and a Beethoven. He understands that the appearance of the house of God is not a matter of indifference, whether it be a fitting structure such as we find in the cathedral of Chartres or in San Marco in Venice, where beauty speaks of God's world, or whether it exudes a desolate and depressing atmosphere like the false Gothic of the eighties. He understands the claim that wherever anything makes Christ known, there nothing can be beautiful enough in the sense of beauty of form. He also understands the significance that beauty of form possesses as a spiritual nourishment even after the redemption. It is not a matter of indifference whether a hymn to the Sacred Heart or to Our Lady be sentimental and trivial, or whether it be of a sublime and exalted beauty like the *Ave verum* by Mozart, for triviality falsifies the world into which we are here to be drawn. Here the liturgy is again our great model. The liturgy of the Mass and of the Breviary, as the prayer of Christ, as a participation of the sacred life of the Church, clearly indicates in its construction, its form, its rhythm, and its Gregorian chant what role beauty of form plays, how it is also fit to speak to us of God, to lead us to God, to glorify God.

No one, perhaps, so clearly recognized the transcendence of the beauty of form and the fact that it is a quintessence of a more exalted world than did the great Cardinal Newman, who also expressed it in these sublime words:

> There are seven notes in the scale; make them fourteen; yet what a slender outfit for so vast an enterprise! What science brings forth so much out of so little? Out of what poor elements does some great master in it create his new world? Shall we say that all this exuberant intensiveness is a mere ingenuity or trick of art like some game

or fashion of the day without reality, without meaning? Or is it possible that that inexhaustible evolution and disposition of notes, so rich yet so simple, so intricate yet so regulated, so various yet so majestic, should be a mere sound which is gone and perishes? Can it be that those mysterious stirrings of the heart, and keen emotion, and strange yearnings after we know not what, and awful impressions from we know not whence, should be brought in us by what is unsubstantial, and comes and goes, and begins and ends in itself? It is not so; it cannot be. No; they have escaped from some higher sphere; they are the outpourings of eternal harmony in the medium of created sound; they are echoes of our home; they are the voice of angels, or the Magnificat of the Saints, or the Living Laws of Divine Governance, or Divine Attributes; something they are besides themselves, which we cannot encompass, which we cannot utter, though mortal man, and he perhaps not otherwise distinguished above his fellows, has the gift of eliciting them. (*University Sermons*, XV)

AESTHETICISM AND THE TRUE DISPOSITION TO ART

Goethe says somewhere that poems are like the colorful windows of a church. From outside they appear black and lackluster, but from within they reveal their colorful beauty and splendor. This is true of the world of art as a whole. There are people who approach art entirely from the outside without the slightest sense for how they must direct their gaze if they are to notice anything in this world. Indeed, we even encounter people who are indignant that things which are obviously unreal are presented in the theater and who lack any understanding for what might

Originally written in German ("Ästhetizismus und künstlerische Einstellung"), this essay is one of Hildebrand's earliest aesthetic writings. First published in 1927 and subsequently included in two German collections of essays by Hildebrand, it has been translated into English here for the first time by John Henry Crosby.

be gained by this. Or they consider our enthusiasm for a painting or a piece of music to be quite exaggerated. They see only a colorful representation of some object and cannot understand what the point of this might be. In the case of music they hear only irritating noise and shake their heads that anyone could take interest in such foolishness.

There is in fact a kind of person for whom the world of beauty and in a particular way the world of art is not just closed off, but for whom this sphere seems like a superfluous luxury, a pastime for aesthetes and dreamers, even if public opinion today causes people to refrain from expressing these views aloud. Such people see the interest in beauty as unhealthy, exaggerated, leading away from the solid ground of reality and incompatible with the seriousness of reality. Beauty strikes them as something unreal, much the way we would think of a hallucination, and our interest in it as an eccentricity that makes them laugh and feel superior. They think they alone remain rooted in what is real and truly important, without losing time on such trifles. We describe this kind of person as a philistine. Material goods necessary for life in a very modest sense of the term, goods without which life in its barest form would be impossible, and also those things that enable a pleasant, comfortable existence seem to them indispensable and worthy of serious pursuit. Any cultural goods, science, art, the beauty of nature, all strike them as frivolous luxuries to the extent that they are not, as is the case with certain branches of science, essential for the production of material goods or for the preservation of life. Their typical worldview is utilitarianism. The value of something in itself, the inner beauty of knowledge, of art, nature, of a human relationship like a noble friendship or a marriage is not sufficient to make something worthy of existing, let alone to bestow it with meaning. To what extent is something useful for life, understood as unfolding in more or less material terms? This is the question that determines the significance of any matter. Anything that cannot be incorporated into this category seems to them like idle play, like superfluous, inessential, purely subjective fantasies of satisfying indulgence.

The philistine is also characterized by the fact that quantity alone, and not quality, seems to him worthy of attention. Quantitative size is capable of impressing him and commanding his admiration; but inner greatness which is given qualitatively he cannot see. There are of course many varieties of philistine, like the more moralistic type filled with *ressentiment* for the world of spiritual goods, or the type who is more coarse, rude, brutish, unsophisticated, among other types. But for what matters in our context, they all have one thing in common: beauty for them has no legitimate place in the world. Interest in beauty, as in any purely spiritual values, aside from certain moral values, strikes them as an unhealthy and unreasonable aestheticism.

Radically opposed to such people are those we describe as aesthetes, in whose lives the fundamental attitude is a certain soft focus on enjoying [*Genusseinstellung*]. They look with contempt at everything that belongs to the sober hierarchy of material goods, to that which, however prosaic, is nevertheless indispensable. The perspective of the useful, they think, should play no role whatsoever; to apply it strikes them as petty and banal. Only the world of aesthetic values accessible only to the select few can impress them. They are even suspicious of the world of moral values, for which they lack a basic sense; they say these are too practical and utilitarian, too bourgeois and obvious. Only the express enjoyment of brilliance, elegance, fineness, of all that is well made, pleasing, perfectly formed, and refined seems to them to make life worth living. They have a certain disdain toward the meaning of reality as such. They are born subjectivists for whom the world is constituted in their sensations. They are hypersensitive to anything earthy and ugly, even when it represents an unavoidable part of human wretchedness and belongs to the tragedy of human existence. Incomparably worse: aesthetes for the most part remain heartless spectators in life, observing everything only from the outside, without responding to the objective demands of the actual situation they are in. Instead of compassion, loving sympathy, and a readiness to offer real help, we find them turning away from everything that appears "unaesthetic." They think themselves too refined and exceptional to say openly in plain words or, rather, to admit to themselves, that they too share in all the poverty of human nature. They are usually characterized by a certain arrogance, a tendency to look down on the uncultivated masses who know nothing of life in its "true and higher" form. As Horace put it, "*Odi profanum vulgus*" ("I hate the common masses").

With this the radical antithesis between the philistine and the aesthete is clearly brought out. What makes life worth living for the one does not exist for the other. Already at first glance we see that both stances are false, that both the aesthete and the philistine represent an unattractive, truncated human type, even if their essential orientations are entirely different.

What, then, is the true role of the world of beauty and that of art in particular? Could it be that the right attitude lies in the middle between that of the philistine and the aesthete? Is there error in both of these types only due to the fact that the one grants the world of beauty too much importance and the other too little? No. The right stance toward the world of beauty and especially of art does not lie between the philistine and the aesthete; rather, it is essentially different from both. Artistic people are not moderate aesthetes. The authentic artistic and the aestheticist attitudes are ultimately diametrically opposed. Only in the eyes of the philistine do they appear identical. We will now attempt to demonstrate their essential and profound difference, indeed their incompatibility, and to unpack the nature of the authentic disposition to art.

I

In order to understand the true disposition to art as such [*künstlerische Einstellung*], we will begin by considering various extra-artistic and inartistic stances that differ sharply from it, though for reasons quite other than aestheticism. From among the great multiplicity of false attitudes toward art, which naturally exceed the boundaries of this essay, we want to focus on three primary kinds:

1. the extra-artistic disposition that is focused purely on the subject matter of art;

2. the extra-artistic disposition that is focused on artistic elements of a formal type;

3. the inartistic disposition that is specifically tasteless in nature.

1. For the first type of extra-artistic person, the only thing that interests them in a work of art, whether a painting or a play, is the thing itself that is represented. Often the description below a paint-

ing communicates the object of their interest more immediately than the image itself. They know and understand nothing of the entirely distinctive language by which the painting conveys and reveals particular worlds of beauty, depth, and lyricism. This is why they search for a meaning that is accessible to them outside the scope of this language, which is communicated through a language that exists entirely outside the realm of art, by that universal language through which an idea is usually conveyed and made vivid to our imagination. Artistic interest is here supplanted by the delight in seeing an event vividly portrayed, whether a historical occurrence or an individual person, which for whatever reason interests the viewer. Such people are lacking in two ways. First, an understanding for the language in which art in various ways, be it visual art, music, or poetry, conveys its specific artistic content and the very particular world of artistic values. Second, the object of their delight and enjoyment is of an entirely different sort. Not only do they pass blindly over the way in which the artistic content is expressed, they cannot even reach the artistic content because they substitute it with something entirely different. Quite understandably, art will not play a great role for such people. If they bother with art at all, it is because they believe it somehow belongs to education or because they take it on faith from others that art involves something beautiful that must be treated with reverence.

The hallmark of this first most primitive type—seeking as a surrogate for real aesthetic values that which elicits a certain delight or enjoyment—is that it privileges the importance that the thing depicted holds for completely other reasons in the mind of the beholder. Let us say such a person sees the statue of Moses by Michelangelo. He does not see the true atmosphere and greatness of this work of art, nor does he even seek its special world and atmosphere along these lines. Knowing of Moses, he is interested in any associations with this name coming to life in a vivid depiction. The form of these associations is not essential in our connection; the decisive thing is that they are extra-artistic in character and thus not focused on the beauty and greatness of the story and of Moses' personality as we encounter it in Sacred Scripture. That would represent a new and complex case, namely, a true artistic disposition on the literary level paired with an inartistic one in the domain of visual art. We are thinking rather of people who possess this primitive extra-artistic attitude toward all domains of art, as we find in visitors to a gallery who are preoccupied by whether the faces of those depicted remind them of people whom they like or dislike. I recall an actual case of a woman who kept saying to her companion as they stood before the pictures, "Now he really doesn't have a pleasant and attractive face. Could you love, let alone marry, such a person?" There is even a kind of pseudo-art in which the artist fully caters to such extra-artistic desires, like in the historical paintings of Karl von Piloty or the novels of Felix Dahn. It need not always be a case of particular associations that a person connects with the subject matter of the artwork. It may simply be a case of a benign romantic delight in discovering in represented form something real that one already knows. This is a very common attitude especially in relation to the visual arts. Being completely blind to the actual atmosphere of a painting, such a person is delighted to see cities, human beings, and landscapes "reproduced," just as he delights in finding the world suddenly shrunk in a miniature display. This delight, which is quite unserious and stems from a romantic curiosity, has nothing to do with a work of art *qua* art; this is clear without further explanation. Such a person has no idea of the new world that art reveals.

We must also mention another much less primitive type of extra-artistic disposition that falls within the first of the three primary types mentioned above, namely, the one preoccupied with the subject matter of a work of art. Here we have people who do not just replace the artistic creation with extra-artistic connections to that which is represented, but who look for a morally valuable or metaphysically significant "idea" as the real essence of the work. While they do not just single out what is represented in the work, like the event depicted in a painting, for example, a historical occurrence or a scene from mythology, but seek to take the work of art as a whole, nevertheless they do not understand the particular language of a given artform and remain insensible to its special world of values. They do not seek the surrogate in various banal connections to the subject but in the sphere of a deep and noble idea, seeking to make use of a faculty that would be suitable in a philosophical essay. Being unable to perceive the special language of art and its particular kind of beauty, one believes something of true value can exist only in the mode of what one otherwise takes to be the archetype of all values, namely, of a sublime idea that can be conceptually formulated and apprehended with the faculty of general intellectual understanding.

2. A completely different kind of extra-artistic attitude, beyond these attempts to find a surrogate for the specific world of art and to reduce the work of art to something extra-artistic, is the interest in the merely formal "well-made" character of an artwork. A more primitive form of this attitude is the interest in the faithful reproduction of what is represented, in how true-to-life a representation is, and indeed for its "achievement" rather than its charm—in portraits, the degree of similarity; in compositions, the ideal that a Greek painter supposedly attained in his painting of harvested grapes such that the birds picked at them; in novels, novellas, and plays, the representation of life, such that we believe ourselves to be on the street, in the train, in society, because people speak "exactly this way" as we know from our frequent experience. What commands naïve admiration is the artist's accomplishment and ability, where "accomplishment" is entirely seen along the lines of any other sort of skillfulness and one remains completely unaware of the specif-

ic meaning of the work of art. A purely auxiliary function of art—the ability to make a detailed and faithful representation of nature (which has no place in music and architecture and has place only in certain artforms, like painting, sculpture, and poetry, and even here is not always required)—is severed from its purely subordinate role, made the primary theme, and, what is more, still misunderstood. Not only does this shift attention from the work of art to the artist—an unhealthy distortion—but the artist's accomplishment is seen under the aspect of an extra-artistic skillfulness; basically, he is more or less placed on the same level as the juggler. People who do this consider themselves to be very artistic because they are abstracting from the subject matter. The subject of artistic treatment makes no difference to them; they simply admire the artist for being able to "reproduce it so well." For such people the real ideal would be reached if the artist could achieve what a photograph attains. The artistic movement that panders to these extra-artistic desires is naturalism.

By contrast, the less primitive form of this formalistic error focuses on whether the artist attains the effect he "intended." It does not measure the accomplishment by the standard of the reproduction of reality but by how close the artist has come to what he "wanted." The actual realization and working out of the intended effect, regardless of what the effect consists in, is the only determining factor. Whether a certain artist wants to highlight the rousing character and elegance of a dance or the specifically trivial and exaggerated atmosphere of an operetta, whether he intends an effect marked by sensationalism and kitsch or wishes to express a situation of true lyricism and mysterious greatness, plays no role for this type of person. All that matters is whether the artist has actually realized what he wanted.

If the more primitive form lays emphasis purely on a certain skillfulness of the artist, merely on ability, then the emphasis here lies more on a formal talent, a certain power of the artist. Totally overlooked is the fact that inartistic intentions may exist and that a completely new sort of talent and power is required to create truly artistic effects, compared with the talent required for merely intense effects. To compose a work like *Figaro* requires not just an incomparably greater talent than for one like *Tosca*, but a talent of a completely different kind, namely, the talent necessary for realizing truly artistic intentions. We find here a relatively greater understanding for the unique language of the work of art than with the type oriented purely toward the subject matter. But an understanding for the unique content of the work of art is absent, and attention is completely shifted from the work to the artist and his achievement. The aspect of talent as such, which delights us even outside the sphere of art, constitutes the surrogate here for the actual value of the work of art.

3. The third kind of inartistic attitude is specifically tasteless and in effect inartistic. One's gaze is not diverted from the work of art to something else; one does not seek the object of one's interest and delight either in purely accidental aspects of the subject matter or in the artist's accomplishment, but in the "content" of the work: on what as a whole it communicates to us, on what its atmosphere and its "world" convey. The problem here is that the object of satisfaction is not artistic value, which leave such people cold, but precisely artistic disvalue. They take pleasure in what is trivial, sentimental, cloyingly tasteless, in cheap effects, in what whips up our craving for the sensational, and they look for these qualities in art. The deep and noble character

of genuine art, which avoids all cheap effects, does not speak to them and is incapable of inspiring them. They do not possess a sensibility for true art and its authentic worlds of beauty. They are not in search of any otherwise thoroughly legitimate interest to make into a surrogate; instead they respond especially to poor works of art that are bearers of triviality—the quality in the artistic sphere that can be described as analogous to "evil" in the moral sphere. Like people who love vulgar, nauseating perfumes and are insensitive to the fragrance of flowers, such inartistic, tasteless people take particular delight in artistically negative values. Naturally, the emotional life of such a person, unlike someone with the above-described extra-artistic disposition, is marked by many negative qualities. These are trivial people, who are marked by sentimentality rather than depth of feeling in their lives as a whole, who are tactless and tasteless in their expressions and feelings. Thus they do not seek in art that which has its legitimate place in life but is not the object of art, like those marked by the extra-artistic attitude, but qualities that in life too represent something negative and perverted. Let us not delude ourselves about the fact that in all spheres of art, by far the majority that is produced is characterized by triviality, sentimentality, cheap and superficial effects, sensationalist titillation, saccharine tastelessness, and that a large part of these qualities are consciously intended and expressly aimed at satisfying these inartistic desires (as in most operettas, serialized novels, detective stories, etc.).

In addition to these three kinds of extra-artistic and inartistic attitudes, I want briefly to point out two attempts of a more theoretical nature that seek to reduce art to a completely extra-artistic function. Many believe that the meaning and value of a work of art consists in the fact that it presents a sharp, vivid expression of the personality of the artist. A work of art is said to be poor if it lacks some such stamp of personality, whether because the work is weak and conventional, or because it is specifically impersonal. What is decisive here is not the qualitative character of the world of an artwork but the formal matter of fact that the work is a real, powerful expression of a personality, without any regard to what sort of values the personality itself possesses. It is clear that the attempt to find a criterion to judge art that can be applied without any real artistic understanding represents a theory that completely misses the nature of art. (This attempt has understandable roots, namely, in those who feel compelled somehow to pass judgment on art, despite lacking a real relationship to art.) Even though a real work of art always simultaneously functions as an expression of a personality, nevertheless this dimension is in no way decisive for the work. To be sure, there is such a thing as the stamp of authentic originality, an expression of true and abundant personality that trivial productions could never possess. A certain dependency on cliché is always characteristic of a trivial and shoddy work—even if this is also the typical expression of a trivial personality. But even the stamp of real originality is not of constitutive significance for whether something is a work of art or not. And this is why it also cannot function as a criterion, for there are creations of the spirit that, while vivid expressions of a rich and original personality, do not, despite their intention, represent a work of art.

It is even easier to arrive at the view that the meaning of a work of art lies in the fact that it represents a vivid expression of its era. One certainly need not possess a sensibility for the real world of art, neither an understanding of its unique language nor its particular values, to establish that something is a vivid expression of a zeitgeist. After all, what matters is whether a given zeitgeist is at all artistic. A lively expression of the 1880s in Germany is not yet a work of art; on the contrary, to the degree that a period is inartistic, so also will the art of that time be inartistic. Even where a zeitgeist is permeated by an artistic culture, such as in antiquity, the Middle Ages, and the Renaissance, the function of being an expression of the zeitgeist is of a secondary character. What ultimately determines the value of any work of art is the world of beauty in which all great art of all eras shares; it is to be sought—notwithstanding the value of any particular cultural world—precisely where Phidias, Giotto, Michelangelo, and Grünewald converge, in what San Marco in Venice, the Trevi Fountain in Rome, the cathedral of Chartres, and the equestrian statue of Frederick III by Andreas Schlüter all have in common.

The artistically disposed person stands in contrast to the extra– and inartistic attitudes and at odds with the just-mentioned futile efforts to conceive of the artistic domain. He has a sensibility for the entirely unique language, which is unlike anything analogous in other cultural domains, through which every work of art, though specifically different in every artistic genre, reveals to us the world of authentic beauty. Above all, he has a sense for the noble, profound world of beauty in itself, which comes to us as the reflection of a higher world. He does not seek the work of art in order to satisfy an interest focused on aspects adhering more or less accidentally in the work, but opens his eyes to the world of value all its own that the artwork reveals as an entity of a very particular kind, an entity whose structure and level of reality is incomparable to the objects we otherwise encounter in life. He does not take interest in a painting because it treats of an event tied to pleasing associations; rather, he is enveloped in the atmosphere that the image radiates through its visual language—the profound, solemn greatness, the mysterious, intense beauty of a painting by Giorgione; the mysterious sublimity and tragic greatness, the ultimate, potent, soul-expanding beauty of Michelangelo's statue of "Night" in his Medici Tombs; the redeemed, heavenly, transfigured beauty and the brilliant, overflowing fullness and greatness of Mozart's opera *Don Giovanni*; the unique world of heroic greatness, mysterious depth, and most radiant of beauty in Beethoven's ninth symphony.

We must now try to clarify what it means to say

that a work of art has a "language of its own" [*eigenen Sprache*]. Let us consider, for example, the adagio from the ninth symphony of Beethoven. The inartistic person, even if he has an ear for music, will look for something that this music is supposed to represent, whether an idea or a human emotion. He will either enjoy this directly or he will focus on the particular accomplishment represented by the expression of these emotions. In either case, he remains insensible to the particular language of music and the unique character of the artistic content. The person with an artistic disposition, by contrast, will grasp the special language of music. He will not search for something else but understand the entirely characteristic and singular way in which even a theme or a melody reveals a world of beauty all its own—that transfigured, luminous, heart-expanding world that a melody as such can reveal and support, not because it "represents" something sublime, a sorrow or a joy, or because it symbolizes an idea, but because it is as it is, while another melody exudes a saccharine atmosphere both trivial and banal. Like the individual melody, a complete entity as unlimited and rich in differentiation as a symphony or an opera reveals an abundance of such artistic worlds, but all in their own particular artistic language, which can be understood only according to its own unique character. Just as music has its own particular artistic language, so every other artistic genre has its own such language.

But important as it is to see that art as such, like every artistic genre, possesses its own language, it is also important is to grasp that it is a language that conveys a particular artistic content and that the language is not an end in itself. The fact that certain artists consider it an inartistic stance even to acknowledge such a content itself betrays a typical inartistic disposition. They think a painting's composition, unity, consistency, certain lighting effects, etc., are ends in themselves and contain the real value; they think a content can consist only in subjective emotional effects that are of no importance. Naturally, this is completely false. I really grasp the autonomy and intrinsic importance of art only when I see that it not only possesses its own language but also a content of its own, which is thoroughly objective and must be fully distinguished from subjective emotional effects. This content, say that of a Mozart theme, does not consist in the feeling it arouses or in the enthusiasm it elicits, but in the totally unique objective qualities of the world of beauty that is revealed and carried by this theme, a world presupposed by our feelings and to which my enthusiasm and being moved are a response. Regardless of how knowledgeable someone is about the brilliance of composition, the use of materials, and so forth, he understands nothing if he does not grasp what a world of poetry, of a unique, hovering gracefulness and golden, luminous beauty suffuses a work like Shakespeare's *As You Like It*; what a world of greatness, momentous historical moments, what an atmosphere of heroism and universality are displayed in a play like Shakespeare's *Julius Caesar*; what a unique classical lyricism, what transfigured light, like an afternoon sun, what a liberating and beautiful world, radiant with ultimate truth, fill Cervantes' *Don Quixote*; what a world of transfigured, heavenly, redeemed beauty Mozart's *Requiem* embodies; what a world of ultimate seriousness and hidden depth fills Beethoven's late quartets.

It is impossible to express in words the particular artistic content of different works of art. What I have been saying by way of descriptions are at most inadequate intimations, for this content allows itself to be expressed only in the particular language of the artwork itself. But this does not prevent the artistic content from existing and from being something fully objective, something that makes up the soul and meaning of the individual work of art, indeed of art itself. The multiplicity of these artistic qualities is immense. Nevertheless, these qualities are all unified in a profound inner way through the fundamental artistic quality of a real beauty, just as moral value qualities, despite a manifold abundance, all belong to the fundamental quality of "good." Certainly brilliance, the specific element of mastery, and perfection are significant factors in the work of art. But ultimately they have a supporting role in relation to the "beautiful world" that a work of art realizes. The world that the work of art conveys and reveals to be a higher reality than itself remains the soul of the artwork. The person who is artistically disposed grasps this world of beauty and understands that it is something all its own, a completely new revelation of God, as it were, which bears a parallel to the revelation found in the moral sphere but to which it cannot be reduced. And for this reason he grasps simultaneously the autonomy of the realm of art as such, in its special language and content, and the real earnestness and dignity of this realm that is anything but a luxury and a pleasant adornment of life. This should not cast any doubt on the fact that the moral sphere of course has a primacy of its own. The world of moral values represents a voice of God that in principle may be heard by anyone, a path to God along which everyone without exception is commanded to walk. This is not the case in the same way in the world of the beautiful and of art. But it does not, as I said, change the fact that the world of the beautiful and of art in particular represent a real voice of God. To understand this voice requires a special sensibility; neither can it be heard by everyone, nor is there an analogous obligation (as in the moral sphere) to tread the special path it indicates.

In describing the world of art as a "world of beauty" we have to remember that beauty can be spoken of with a great variety of meanings. There is a kind of one-dimensional beauty that must be described more as the beauty of a material, a type of beauty that is limited to being pleasing thanks to its harmonious quality. A higher world of infinite depth is not revealed in this kind of beauty, which is also accessible to the inartistic person. He takes delight in the beauty of the new green grass he sees when walking, the beauty of a blue lake, a tall cliff, or a well-proportioned face. But of the profound worlds of beauty contained within nature, such as in the unique poetry and classical, transfigured beauty of Italy, he surmises nothing. He sees only the beauty that, so to speak, is merely a material quality. From this peripheral sort of beauty we must completely distinguish the beauty that can be described as the fragrance of all that is really valuable. We find such beauty poured out over a person who is truly pure and humble, pervaded by love and kindness, a beauty reflected in her face—that victorious light and radiance, broadening our hearts, that emanates from every real virtue the moment we see it clearly, and that we see radiating in its highest perfection in the figure of a saint like St. Elizabeth or St. Teresa. This is the beauty that grips our heart with longing when we look from the Capitol across the Forum into the Roman countryside and the distant Alban Hills; the beauty that reveals itself in every glorious sunset; the beauty that is the manifestation of the good and true, the "face" of the world of values, the appearance of the truly valuable; the deep, true beauty that is not an accidental trait but, when it appears, reveals the higher, truer, realer world of the totality of values—all this we can call beauty of the second power, in contrast to the one-dimensional material beauty described above. Now it is this beauty that makes up the domain of value proper to art: not a beauty that is a wistful romantic view into an unreal world of the imagination, nor one that leads into a flimsy, anemic world of abstract ideals, but one at whose appearance the victorious reality of the world of authentic values stands before us, because it is a reflection of what is most real, namely, the absolute and self-subsisting being, God Himself.

Art represents a sphere in which this beauty is the decisive factor that brings together the elements of a work of art into a unified whole. The work of art *qua* artwork exists only in the sphere of the visible and audible; its only task is to realize in its own manner a world of beauty or, put another way, to open a window into the world of this beauty. This distinguishes it, say, from beauty in nature or from the inner beauty of a personality, where beauty is not the formative principle by which a given object is organized.

Now this world of values that real art conveys to us is a world qualitatively all its own within the sphere of aesthetic values. But it is not a world that on principle can be communicated to us only by art, a world that nature, say, cannot also convey. A landscape can be filled with the same lyrical world as a Goethe poem like "Mailied"; a sunset can convey the same world of beauty, filled with yearning and the promise of glory, as a piece of music is able. But only an artistic gaze is able to discover these worlds within nature.

Inartistic people see in nature, so to speak, only beautiful material. They see a sparkling river or the fresh green of spring, and so forth, but a part of nature does not suddenly form a unity of the sort that could bear a lyrical world or serve as home of a particular beauty. They see only individual things, trees, mountains, forests, but cannot see the mysterious relationships among different contents by which an individual thing in nature stands forth and becomes incorporated into an inner and more encompassing unity, the bearer of a special atmosphere, and possessed of a particular countenance. But artistic people see the individual things that form an artistic whole in nature and so are able to discern the values in nature that make up the soul of art. This in no way affects the irreducibility of art to nature. At first it is the artist alone who sees these deeper worlds of beauty that are hidden in nature and in life; he is then able to realize them in a work of art in such a way that reveals them to people whose eyes do not penetrate as deeply as his. Every real work of art, beyond its own intrinsic worth, also has the function of unveiling nature and life as bearers of these worlds of beauty.

II

The authentic artistic disposition recognizes that art has its own sphere that does not derive its importance from any other domain, while at the same time respecting the great seriousness and dignity of the world of values contained within art. Now the attitude of the aesthete is distinguished from the artistic disposition along totally different lines from those of the extra– and inartistic dispositions treated above. The aesthete can in principle have a sensibility for the specific language of art and can also, as we said, possess thoroughly good taste. There are aesthetes who are interested in unquestionably genuine works of art and who reject trivial, saccharine, and sentimental things. The crucial shortcoming in such people is not primarily a lack in specifically artistic inclination as in their general stance toward values.

This is why the extent to which they have good taste is ultimately immaterial to their character as aesthetes, that is, how much of a sensibility they have for a given artistic genre. The inartistic element in their disposition lies in the enjoyment-oriented, irreverent, unserious, unobjective fundamental stance toward the world, which necessarily conceals from them the ultimate seriousness and the nature of artistic values, even if in principle they possess an artistic sensibility. They approach the world of values only as an object of enjoyment in the precise sense of the term, rather than entering into this world with reverent abandonment and enthusiasm. They treat the work of art like a meal whose flavor melts in their mouth. To fully understand the nature of this enjoyment-oriented attitude, we must briefly reflect on the sphere in which this approach to pleasure is most appropriate.

There are goods meant for our use in which we stand in a position of sovereignty, things such as food and drink, clothing, tools, means of transportation, etc. That such goods, which have a specific serving function in our lives, are subordinated to us is obvious. Not only are they clearly available for our use, but the pleasure they give us, like the enjoyment of a meal, is something that we can enjoy but to which we cannot reverently devote ourselves. We remain the master of that which we use and enjoy. By contrast, there are also goods whose objective value commands reverence and humble enthusiasm, such as the beauty of nature, art, of noble persons with whom we are in community, or of a morally noble deed that we are permitted to witness. What first stands out among these goods is that, contrary to those previously mentioned, simply their existence is gladdening, even prior to any closer contact we may come into with them. They do not have a serving function in our lives, they are not here for our use, and we are not in a sovereign role in relation to them. The noble person whom I may call my friend is indeed a great gift for me, but a gift in relation to which I stand in reverent gratitude and whose meaning does not primarily lie in being there for me. Certainly, it is a great gift to experience a work of art, but the world of beauty it reveals to me, which fills me with yearning and draws me upward, is not important just because it makes me happy; on the contrary, it can make me happy only because it reveals to me a higher reality within it that is independent of me. It is not difficult to see that these two attitudes, which are fitting for these two kinds of goods, are so different as to be totally opposed to one another.

Now enjoyment in the precise sense of the term is an attitude in which we do not look upon an object and immerse ourselves in its values, as in the case of enthusiasm, but in which we consciously enjoy and exhaust the pleasure offered to us by the object. An example that epitomizes enjoyment is found, for example, in the gourmet who allows food to melt in his mouth, relishing all the pleasure of a pleasant taste, slowly savoring and exhausting it. There is always something unpleasant, unattractive, and dangerous in such a pursuit of enjoyment; yet with food and drink, indeed with all goods that are intended for our use, it does not represent a deformation that would prevent us from accessing the content of these goods. If I enjoy a dish in this manner, its taste is not concealed to me.

But such a posture of enjoyment in relation to goods that call for reverent devotion from me is a complete perversion. If I seek to enjoy in this sense the happiness that a friendship affords me, this egocentric focus on my happiness, this turning away from the object whose existence is the wellspring of my happiness, this flippant, unserious self-seeking would seal off the true value of the gift for me and so also dissolve the true, profound happiness that flows from the gift. At most, it is possible to "enjoy" in this way the vain satisfaction of having a friend who is a person of high standing. Similarly, to enjoy art and all bearers of real beauty in this way represents a completely perverse attitude. To the person who wants to let the music of Mozart or a sculpture of Michelangelo "melt in his mouth," so to speak, who treats such works of art as if they were caviar or sweet wine, true beauty is necessarily concealed, with only a feast for the ears and eyes remaining. While his eyes pass over the work of art without really understanding it, he himself remains the focus, rather than being raised out of himself into the sanctuary of the work.

Now this conscious savoring is the characteristic fundamental stance of the aesthete, while the soul of the true artistic disposition lies in the reverent humble surrender of self, in being truly moved and profoundly gladdened in such a way that one forgets oneself and does not seek one's own pleasure.

We can now understand why the aesthete remains trapped in a fundamentally peripheral relation to art and to the world of beauty, despite the fact that he seems to grant them such an exclusive and unique role, which at bottom he grants not to beauty but to his own sensations and enjoyment. He and the satisfaction of his needs form the center of the world. We can see clearly how the aesthete's focus on enjoyment—unobjective, irreverent, flippant—is to blame for all the perversions that typify his stance toward the world. Even if he has good taste, this stance leads him to stray from what is essential in a work of art and get stuck in what is inessential and peripheral because this alone permits itself to be enjoyed in this manner. The elegant, formally successful, sophisticated, masterful, spirited—these alone he will see in a good artwork; and also, as is common today, he will enjoy what is primitive for its primitivity, the incoherent for its incoherence, imbalance in form as an especially refined rarity. Or he will savor the purity of style, the expression of a fine culture in a work of art—in Mozart, say—artistically misunderstanding him completely, appreciating him as model of Rococo culture without grasping anything of the time-transcending, truly transfigured, moving and triumphant beauty and greatness of Mozartean music.

The aesthete aims at skimming off the cream, so to say. He is never really moved and overcome, and so he necessarily shifts his gaze from the artistic to certain peripheral aesthetic qualities that one can be interested in without understanding anything of art. Above all this stance cuts off the whole depth dimension of art. But we can also understand how the aesthete comes to this false isolation of art, to this recognition of aesthetic values alone. The person with an artistic disposition is entirely free of this isolation, even though he recognizes clearly the unique language of art and the totally irreducible value of beauty and its ultimate seriousness.

Moral values should not be enjoyed in this sense. Someone who perceives the world egocentrically only as a possible stimulus for his pleasure, whether crude or more refined, and who is interested in the world only as a possible object of enjoyment cannot even begin to make sense of the world of moral values. Such a person cannot even misunderstand beauty. How could one, in the precise sense of the term, enjoy the kindness, the readiness to forgive out of love, the purity, and the humility of another person? With this we come to a further and highly important characteristic. The aesthete, due to his enjoyment-oriented attitude, is specifically unobjective, that is, he does not look at what in a given situation is of central importance, at what is "thematic," at what constitutes the meaning of a given situation. Let us say he is present at an accident. Rather than being filled with deep pity and thinking only of what alone is important, namely, to help the injured, he flees from such an "unaesthetic" sight. Or let us say he witnesses a catastrophic fire. Rather than being shaken by the terrible event, he enjoys the tremendous spectacle. In the event of a robbery, he enjoys the aesthetic allure of the thief's cunning, his power and audacity, the elegance with which he carries out his deeds, rather than being indignant at his depravity, which in reality of course is also extremely ugly, and rather than having compassion for his unfortunate soul. The cold heartlessness and superficiality of the aesthete emerge clearly. He sees everything fundamentally from the outside and does not enter in to the values and disvalues that are decisive and thematic in a given situation. This separates him from reality in a profound way. The world for him is a façade. He clings to externals inasmuch as he adheres to what is inessential in a given sphere. It is this same unobjective stance that he also has toward art.

He remains attached to peripheral aesthetic aspects and fundamentally does not understand the central thematic meaning represented by this sphere, just as he does not understand it in the case of moral values and in life. All that counts for him are aesthetic values and art, not because he really grasps the actual profound value qualities of this sphere, but because here at least he can exercise his misunderstanding, his distorted interpretation, and reduce everything to certain peripheral aesthetic values, which he is able to enjoy, without becoming conscious of being at odds with what the situation requires.

Ultimately, a certain self-indulgence lurks in all aestheticism. One enjoys the feeling of being refined and exceptional, because in dealing with exceptional works of art one imagines oneself to be participating in their exceptional character. This is why the aesthete sets his sights precisely on these higher sources of enjoyment. He does not want just any pleasure; he wants refined pleasure in things that impart to him the consciousness of being cultivated and exceptional. Among aesthetes the vital sphere is usually not well developed. People with hearty appetites are seldom aesthetes. The particular accent on refinement and on this self-indulgence give the aesthete a certain soft and weakly quality that prevents us from ultimately taking such types seriously. The aesthete, like any other type defined by enjoyment, is a miserable and unserious figure, not for his emphasis on aesthetic value but for his focus on enjoyment, his imprisonment in an unobjective Epicurean world, his clinging to what is secondary in all situations, and his looking at things merely from without.

None of this finds any place in the authentic stance toward art. Here a person does not look toward himself in any way, but in objective surrender to the work of art is raised beyond himself. It is finally time to abandon the completely false notion that art and its pursuit have the effect of softening us and crippling our will. On the contrary! The truly artistic stance, the capacity to grasp in its full seriousness and metaphysical significance the world of beauty, and of art in particular, the enthusiasm for this world, the ability to be deeply moved and made happy by a true work of art—all this flows from the same fundamental value-responding attitude from which the surrender to the moral good also originates. The artistically disposed person is oriented to what is central within art, to what is of decisive importance in this sphere, while ignoring all the accidental things to which the aesthete remains attached. Being attuned to what is objectively important in the artistic sphere and having a genuine, reverent, value-responding fundamental attitude, the artistic person is much more disposed to grasping and devoting himself to what is essential and decisive in other (non-aesthetic) spheres. In every context he will orient himself toward objective value, and thus in the moral sphere he will recognize moral values as being normative; the only beauty that will captivate and concern him in the moral sphere will be that radiating from real virtue. When called actively to intervene, he will not cling to the aesthetic hue of a situation, which it possesses for someone who sees it from outside, but will decisively step in to help. He will also apprehend the much deeper aesthetic countenance of the situation, which is revealed only to the person who comprehends it from within. Naturally, the artistic disposition alone does not guarantee that someone will look at the world of moral values in this way; much else is needed. But the artistic disposition originates from the same fundamental attitude from which the moral derives and so, if pursued to its ultimate consequences, leads to the moral sphere rather than away from it. Rightly understood, this genuine and ultimate beauty purifies one's heart as it elevates it to God. To be captivated by this beauty does not represent an unhealthy departure from the substantial core of the world, nor an unreal existence in a world of illusion. For this beauty is the countenance of all that is truly valuable in the various spheres of reality, opening our eyes to truth.

Although art is a world all its own, and although beauty represents a value in its own right that prohibits any artificial reduction of art to something else and any dissolution of beauty into other things, beauty does not somehow hang in the air but is incorporated organically into the overall realm of values. Just as God, the fullness of all goodness and truth, is also the epitome and wellspring of all beauty and addresses us through all that is truly beautiful, so also the artistic disposition is in no way a separation from morality and all other values. Rather, it is a stance that makes our hearts more receptive to the voice of God whenever it may speak to us. And so let us conclude with the words of a man who vividly embodies the power of beauty to lead us to God—with the words of Michelangelo:

"Beauty was given to me at my birth as the true model for my dual calling. It is both a light and a mirror for me in both artforms. Whoever thinks otherwise is mistaken. For beauty alone inspires me to envision the sublimity of the conceptions I undertake to paint and sculpt. While insolent and foolish people concoct a false notion of beauty, reducing it to the level of their senses, beauty comes from heaven and will lead any sane spirit to the place from which it came."

INTRODUCTION TO *AESTHETICS*

> Give me a lover and he feels what I am saying: give me one who yearns, give me one who hungers . . . give me one like this, and he knows what I am saying. But if I speak to one who is cold, he does not know what I am saying.
>
> –St. Augustine

Some things can be approached only with great reverence, for it is only then that they disclose themselves to us as they truly are. One of these is beauty. It is of course true that the philosophical analysis of

In his last years, Dietrich von Hildebrand produced a magisterial two-volume *Aesthetics* in German. The Hildebrand Press has published an English translation of the entire work (2016, 2019), made by John F. Crosby, Brian McNeil, and John Henry Crosby. This is the Introduction to volume I, with only the footnotes omitted.

beauty demands a genuine sobriety and the thirst for truth that is required by philosophical *eros*; but this analysis also requires us to approach beauty with reverence, indeed with love. Beauty kindles love, and only the one who remains captivated by it, only the one who is intoxicated by it, only the one who remains a lover while he is investigating its essence, can hope to penetrate its essence.

Plato, Saints Augustine, Anselm, and Bonaventure have repeatedly insisted on the importance of our inner disposition with regard to something, if we wish to get to know it truly. In chapter 1 of his *Proslogion* Saint Anselm writes that without prayer there is no access to a philosophical knowledge of God. We need not approach beauty on our knees, but we must be reverent and receptive, listening in all humility.

The subject of this book is purely philosophical. We ask the ancient Platonic question: *ti esti,* "What is it?", with reference to the essence of beauty, to the basic forms of beauty, and to the whole realm of the beautiful.

This book is neither a history of aesthetics nor a debate with everything that others have said in the past about the sphere of the beautiful. My aim is simply to work out the essence of beauty and of aesthetic values, and I shall refer to earlier insights into the aesthetic sphere and to erroneous theses about it only when we are helped, by the critical assessment of them, to work out the truth of the matter.

Some theses, such as any kind of relativism, get the essence of beauty wrong from the beginning, and interpret beauty as a merely subjective feeling. We need not discuss all of these in detail, but we must thoroughly refute what is common to them all, and we must do this with reference to one or the other author. For it is impossible to separate the formulation of truth from the refutation of error.

Our primary aim is to gain knowledge of genuine essential relations. In the realm of the beautiful, in the aesthetic sphere, there are many matters that are accessible only to philosophical insight and to the philosophical method of investigation, even though they do not possess the character of absolute necessity. This is the necessity found in typical essential laws, such as 2 + 2 = 4; color presupposes extension; moral values cannot belong to impersonal beings; responsibility presupposes freedom. Josef Seifert has written of this distinction between different kinds of essential laws in the introduction to his book *Leib und Seele*.

In this introduction I should like to point out the existential urgency and relevance of an investigation of the true essence of beauty. Beauty is of fundamental importance for the human person, but this is not the primary perspective from which we will look at beauty. Above all, beauty is a reflection of God, a reflection of His own infinite beauty, a genuine value, something that is important-in-itself, something that praises God. This means that the question of the contribution that beauty makes to human life is secondary. Nevertheless, this question is highly significant, since it is extremely important to understand the central objective good that the existence of beautiful things is for the human person. And from the perspective of the ecology of the spirit, it is necessary for us to grasp that the elimination of poetry from life, the destruction of the beauty of nature and especially of the beauty of architecture, terribly impoverishes human existence, and indeed damages and undermines it. We proceed now to point to the fundamental significance of beauty for the human person for his happiness, his character, his moral growth, and his spiritual development.

Beauty as a central source of human happiness

The role of beauty for human happiness is not restricted to those moments in which one is consciously looking at beautiful things. Beauty is active even at those times when one's attention is directed to completely different things. The beauty of the environment in which one lives—one's house, even if it is very simple, like the farmhouses in Tuscany; the view from one's house, both near and far; the architectural beauty of the neighboring houses; the beauty of the sun that shines into the house, and of the shadow cast by a tree—all this nourishes the soul even of the simplest man or woman, entering into their pores even when they are not concentrating on it. And this applies to every situation in life. In the past when a person worked with his hands, bought and sold in the market, and celebrated feasts, he was surrounded by the poetry of these existential situations. This poetry nourished him. He no doubt lacked the understanding of poetry that a poet has when he observes these situations and consciously enjoys them. The simple person did not look at these situations but took them for granted, living in them unselfconsciously. Their poetry nourished his spirit, irrespective of how far he consciously grasped it.

One should not make the mistake of assuming that because many people today apparently lack any sensitivity to beauty, beauty is not a fundamental source of happiness, even for the simplest people. One should not forget the role that beauty plays for the happiness of people—of all people. The atrophy of this sensitivity is a terrible loss, and this ought not to be interpreted as a progress that modern man has made in the industrialized world. We should instead seek to understand the consequences for man of the withdrawal of this spiritual nourishment. The fact that one does not know the causes of a sickness is no proof that one is not sick.

People have grown accustomed to the elimination of the poetry of the world, to the mechanization of life, to the expulsion of beauty; but this does not make any less real the influence on human happiness of this destruction of the charm of an organic, truly human life. People have grown accustomed today to the din to which they are exposed on the street and at home by the many machines that they use; but this does not mean that our nerves escape unscathed from all this cacophony.

It is easy to see the great decrease in human happiness today, and the great increase in the number of psychopaths, suicides, crimes, disorders, revolutions, protests, etc. Are these not unambiguous symptoms of unhappiness, of an unfulfilled hunger for happiness? Why, for example, are the people in Spain so much happier than the people in the United States, although they are much poorer and their life is much less comfortable? They sing while they work, they adorn their simple houses with flowers, and their faces have a happy expression, especially in Andalusia. They are joyful as they gather on the street in the evening, and one cannot fail to see their delight in life and their vitality. As yet there has been little industrialization in the country in which they live. The organic rhythm of life and the poetry of life still survive there to some extent, and very little of the beauty has been destroyed.

There can be no doubt that beauty is one of the great sources of joy in human life. Naturally, like all the central sources of joy, it has many gradations, in accordance with the receptivity of the individual.

No one with eyes to see will deny that the love between husband and wife is one of the greatest sources of happiness in human life. There can be no doubt that a great truth finds expression in the words of Schiller in the "Ode to Joy" ("Whoever calls even only *one* soul *his own*, let him join in the exultation! But let anyone who never achieved this, slink away weeping from our brotherhood!") and of Goethe in *Egmont* ("Only the soul that loves is happy"). Naturally, however, the potential for love varies tremendously from one individual to another. One man can love more deeply, more strongly, and more faithfully than another. He can feel more deeply than another the sweet bliss of a love that is requited, the unheard-of gift of gazing into the eyes of a beloved person. But this does not prevent love from being one of the deepest sources of joy for all human persons. This is true not only of the love between husband and wife, but of love as such, be it the love of friends, of parents for their children or of children for their parents, or the other forms of love. And it applies in an incomparably superior manner to the love for God, the love for Christ.

In the same way, the degree and depth of the happiness caused by beauty has many gradations in different persons. But this does not keep beauty from being a great source of happiness for anyone who is not completely obtuse. Even children are delighted by the beauty of nature, by the poetry of the various seasons of the year, by sunrise and sunset.

The significance of beauty for the development of personality

Beauty is not only a central source of joy. It also possesses a great significance for the development of personality, especially in a moral sense. Plato writes: "At the sight of beauty the soul grows wings." Genuine beauty liberates us in many ways from the force of gravity, drawing us out of the dull captivity of daily life. At the sight of the truly beautiful we are freed from the tension that urges us on toward some immediate practical goal. We become contemplative, and this is immensely valuable. We expand, and even our soul itself becomes more beautiful when beauty comes to meet us, takes hold of us, and fires us with enthusiasm. It lifts us up above all that is base and common. It opens our eyes to the baseness, impurity, and wickedness of many things. Ernest Hello makes a very profound point when he says: "The mediocre person has only one passion, namely hatred of the beautiful." Beauty is the archenemy of mediocrity.

The appreciation of beauty, the interest in beauty, the longing for beauty, the need of beauty—all this has often been seen as a danger for the full understanding of moral values and their ultimate seriousness, or else as something effeminate, something only for aesthetes.

This is to confuse true sensitivity for beauty, true love for all bearers of genuine beauty, with aestheticism, which is a perversion with dangerous effects on the moral quality of the personality. Aestheticism undermines the personality and robs it of its ultimate seriousness. The aesthete does not in any way do justice to the true mystery of beauty and to the message from God that beauty contains. He does not understand that beauty is a value, and so he treats beautiful things as if they were only subjectively gratifying. Kierkegaard calls the unserious playfulness of the aesthete, his coldness and self-centeredness, the "aesthetic attitude," which he contrasts with the ethical sphere and *a fortiori* with the religious sphere. This attitude has nothing in common with receptivity to beauty, with being affected by beauty, or with the value-response to beautiful things. Both Kant and Schopenhauer, each in his own way, saw the nobility that lies in the contemplation of the beautiful and in the love of beautiful things. And Herbart went so far as to regard ethics as a subdivision of aesthetics.

Without discussing this thesis in detail here, let me affirm unambiguously that beauty does in fact have an ennobling effect. Contact with an environment permeated by beauty not only offers real protection against impurity, baseness, every kind of letting oneself go, brutality, and untruthfulness; it has also the positive effect of raising us up in a moral sense. It does not draw us into a self-centered pleasure where our only wish is to indulge ourselves. On the contrary, it opens our hearts, inviting us to transcendence and leading us *in conspectu Dei* ("before the face of God"), before the face of God. Naturally, this last point applies above all to the high, exalted beauty that Kant calls the "sublime" [*das Erhabene*] and that he contrasts with the "beautiful." But even in little things that are charming and graceful, even in the more modest beautiful things, one can find a trace of the pure and the noble. This may perhaps not lead us *in conspectu Dei*, but it does fill us with gratitude to God. It frees us from captivity in our egoistic interests and undoes the fetters of our hearts, releasing us (even if only for a short time) from the wild passions that convulse them.

The distinction between beauty and luxury

There also exists a pseudo-democratic antipathy against beauty, an attitude full of resentment: beauty is regarded as luxury for the elite in society, as an antisocial indulgence that ignores urgent social problems. Luxury, we are told, is morally negative; we must fight against it and abolish it.

A first point: beauty in general, beauty as such, is confused here with refined culture. Obviously, it is ignorant nonsense to regard the beauty of the blue sky in the sunshine, of the mountains, of the sea, of the springtime, summer, fall, and winter, of morning, noon, and evening, or the beauty of architectonic forms (even when these are very simple) as a luxury for the social elite.

Let us think, by contrast, of a really cultivated atmosphere, of the beauty of a noble house with high-quality furniture, curtains, and carpets. This is not in the least "luxurious." It is instead a kind of beauty that presupposes a certain level of culture, a special artistic gift that enables one to create the beauty, and a refined taste in order to appreciate it and enjoy it to the full. The term "elite" may in some sense be appropriate here, but this kind of beauty is no luxury. It therefore retains both its value and its *raison d'être*.

Above all, however, we must explain the true meaning of "luxury." This term is used with three distinct meanings, each of which denotes something devoid of value, unnecessary, superfluous.

1. The first meaning of the word derives from an incorrect use of the term. Anything that is not useful (in the narrowest sense of this word) is considered superfluous. This is due to an ambiguity in the word "superfluous." On the one hand, it means that from a practical, utilitarian perspective something is not required. In this case, the word does not imply that something is valueless, unserious, or dilettantish. The opposite is true: culture as a whole (in contrast to civilization) is "superfluous" in this sense, as is beauty. Beauty is a pure gift, a superfluity (literally, an "overflowing") in the highest sense of the word. Beauty may well be called unnecessary, if one equates "necessary," "serious," and "entitled to exist" with "indispensable in order to achieve a practical goal." Something that is "superabundant" in this sense clearly possesses a high value and is not in any sense a luxury. It is not at all acceptable to apply

the term "luxury" to everything that is superfluous in the sense of superabundant; it reveals a blindness to values, a purely utilitarian attitude, a radical philistinism. To call such things luxury is, as I said, to extend the concept to embrace the totality of culture, the world of beauty, and even moral values, that is, things that are much more important, more necessary, and more serious than all those things that are merely useful. This is a typical instance of an unjustified term that is essentially flawed, indeed based on a contradiction: it takes something that is profoundly meaningful and absolutely necessary, and calls it superfluous and unnecessary.

2. Where, however, the term "luxury" is applied to things that serve only an exaggerated comfort, things that are agreeable but have no inherent value whatever and need not be used from the perspective of usefulness, we are justified in calling them superfluous and in speaking of luxury. Many "beauty products," chairs, carpets, etc., are neither beautiful nor necessary for our daily lives. In other words, they have no inherent aesthetic value and they are superfluous from the practical perspective of achieving goals, that is to say, they are a sheer luxury, especially when they are also expensive. (The concept of

luxury includes the idea that something is expensive.)

3. The term "luxury" has a third meaning, this one referring to quantity. Like the second meaning, this third one refers to something real. This sense of luxury does not assume that the object is not a bearer of value; superfluity is present not due to worthlessness, but to the fact that something is present in a quantity wholly disproportionate to its actual use. If someone has fifty neckties instead of ten, this is clearly a luxury; the same is true of one who has a hundred pairs of shoes or two hundred different dresses, irrespective of how aesthetically valuable they all may be. This is luxury, firstly, because someone possesses much more of such things than he can use, no matter how elegant he might wish to appear. A superfluity of this kind is literally meaningless. Secondly, this superfluity is luxury because it is very expensive and entails an irresponsible relationship to money. There is something disgusting about it and extremely antisocial. To squander money in such a meaningless manner is immoral.

This type of luxury does, however, presuppose that these things are in fact destined to be used. The situation is completely different where someone owns a hundred valuable paintings; it would be meaningless to speak here of luxury. Only those who are well-off can afford aesthetically noble, cultivated furnishings, since these cost a great deal of money. But this is no luxury, since such furnishings have a high value of their own. Their legitimacy is therefore unquestionable, even if only a small number of persons can enjoy them.

We are interested primarily in the difference between such special beauty, which we may say is for the social elite (without thereby disputing its legitimacy or classifying it as luxury), and beauty in general, which is accessible to all and is a highly significant objective good for the person.

Aesthetic experience as "distinterested" and anti-pragmatic

Beauty has a special significance for the spiritual development of the person. In the act of looking at the beautiful—I have in mind here the conscious concentration on something that is beautiful—there lies a special form of the act of self-transcendence, a certain contemplative objectivity. I have frequently pointed to the gesture of transcendence that is contained in every value-response. Here I want to point to one special dimension of this transcendence which belongs specifically to the value-response to the beautiful. Kant aims at this in speaking about the "disinterestedness" [*Uninteressiertheit*] of aesthetic experience. I want to refer here to the thing that Kant saw and that he probably intended to describe, although he did not in fact give an unambiguous explanation of the term "disinterestedness," and indeed failed to distinguish it from a false interpretation.

The objectivity that I envisage lies in the fact that our own person is not always included in a special way in the experience, as in the case of moral value-response. This inclusion applies especially to all morally obligatory actions, in which we reflect consciously not only on the value of the good that we are dealing with, but also on its moral significance, that is, on the rightness of my moral conduct. This is not true of the response to beauty. Another pointer to the existence of a special dimension of self-transcendence is the fact that all value-responses to the beautiful are of a purely contemplative nature, whereas in moral value-response the decisive role is mostly played by the will (and in many cases, by action).

Every genuine value-response is disinterested in

the sense that the person does not seek his own advantage, but gives himself over to the importance that the good possesses in itself. In one sense this transcendence attains its high point in the value-response to morally relevant goods. I have described in detail the various dimensions of transcendence in my book *The Nature of Love*, especially chapter 4.

The beautiful can attract us and make us happy, but its importance is inherently and specifically anti-pragmatic. It penetrates very little into the realm of our own interests, whether into the practical conduct of our lives, our relationships and conflicts with other people, or the way we earn our daily bread. In this way beauty is a typical representative of the valuable, that is, of that which all genuine values possess, of that which characterizes them as values.

This, however, shows us the seriousness and importance of beauty, and it is for this reason that aesthetics, the exact philosophical analysis of the realm of beauty, is an important part of philosophy. And as we have seen, it takes on a particular relevance today.

In this book, I shall attempt to present an aesthetics that keeps its distance to all constructions, that does justice to the essence of beauty and of all aesthetic values, and seeks to penetrate their essence, without taking for granted unexamined theories.

As I have already mentioned, this book is not a debate with already existing theories about beauty, but an analysis of the essence of the world of the beautiful. I should like to repeat Aristotle's words in the *De Anima* (412a), which I have quoted in my *Ethics*: "Let us now make a completely new beginning and attempt to give an exact answer to the question: 'What is the soul?'" We propose to apply this to beauty.

www.ingramcontent.com/pod-product-compliance
Lightning Source LLC
LaVergne TN
LVHW020048110826
845155LV00029B/692